Journey of a Child's Faith
Based on Bible Stories

Children's Poetry
VOL-1

Written By
Sabinah Adewole

Illustrated By
Sanghamitra Dasgupta

Edited by:- Patsy Middleton

Introduction -

The Beginning -08 th March 2020
I was in church today, and God spoke to me about writing Christian poetry for a Child.
I had seen a cross created by a child and informed my older son who was sitting next to me 'I could write about that .....'
Shortly afterwards a group of three children came to light candles confirming what
God was speaking to me in church today ...sometimes God gives you a sign....
My brother in law had asked me before, months ago when are you going to write a faith book? so this is a new journey for me .
My pastor Tunde Ajayi Akinsulire has inspired the idea of a Faith book and I want to give him thanks for the insight he embedded in me.
-
This book cover themes of Innocence, Love, Envy, Leadership, Humility, Compassion,Wisdom, Self -worth, Trust, Lust , Humour, Protection, Jealousy, Faith, Overcoming Temptations, Leadership, Wickedness, Vengeance, Healing, Discipline, Precious amongst others

These Values would help any Child or Adult connect to their inner being and would help them focus on the present towards their growth journey.

#Faithpoetry
#Christianpoet
#Childrenfaithbook
#Faithjourney

ABOUT THE BOOK

This book is a beautifully illustrated introduction on teaching the Bible through Poetry Most of the stories are connected to children. This book uses beautiful imagery helps prepare children and their parents for themes of Innocence, Love, Envy, Leadership, Humility, Compassion, Wisdom, Self -worth, Trust, Lust , Humour, Protection, Jealousy, Faith, Overcoming Temptations, Leadership, Wickedness, Vengeance, Healing, Discipline, Preciousness amongst others

Fun and Easy to read, use this book to encourage your Child on their faith journey, A moral lesson after each poem to give a clearer understanding of the bible message.
Each moral lesson would help your child learn the Values based in each story.

This book is for a Child or Adult to help connect to their inner being and would help them focus on their present faith journey towards a much deeper understanding.

No Copyright Infringement Is Intended

CONTENTS

CONTENTS

………………………………………   …………………………………………

1

The Resurrection of Jesus #01

As I sat in the church
My eyes catch the image of the cross on the wall.
The resurrection of Jesus comes to mind.
Two angels or sinners on each side of the cross.
The image of a well in the picture signifies
growth.
The image of hills, birds and sun implies there is life
after death.Jesus died on the cross for me and you so we
can live and never die.
God raised Jesus after his crucifixion as first of the dead
starting his exalted life as Christ.
The Resurrection of Jesus

Moral message
Jesus is the powerful son of God, who has conquered
death and reigns as Lord of all. (Romans 1:4) Jesus blood
of the new covenant saves his people from their sins.

Composed at home on 09/03/20
Inspired to write about the cross in Church

3

The Birds of the air #02

We went to St Raphael's park in Gidea park.
It was international women's day.
We saw children in the park with their families
We normally feed the swans, ducks,
and birds on the lake with bread.
As we walked we saw a sign on a tree:
You may only feed the birds with grains,
veggies and pellets.
Apparently this food is better for them than bread.
Do we feed on the right spiritual food?
In the bible Birds are described as strengths of hope,
omen or oracle
Life is more important than food, the body more
important than clothes
Birds of the air do not sew or reap or store food away in
barns .Yet your Heavenly Father feeds them.

Moral Message
So the message to us is Be rest assured that God will
take care of your needs

Composed at home on 09/03/20
Inspired to write about the Birds in the park

5

Let the children come into me #03
#from Matt 19:14

As I sat on the train a boy and his dad came on board
As Jesus was preaching the disciples were taking the
children away
But Jesus asked them to bring them to him.
Jesus wants us to have the heart of a child.
In order to enter the kingdom of God
we must have Innocence, and humility.
The kingdom belongs to those who are like these children.
These are the virtues
and they are the greatest in the kingdom of heaven.
This is what the bible teaches.
What does being humble mean to you?
Some 2000 years ago Jesus recorded:
"Whoever takes the lowly position of this child
is the greatest in the kingdom of heaven."

Moral message
The scripture compares believers to Children (Luke 10:21)
whoever takes the low position of this child
is the greatest in the kingdom of heaven.

Composed on the train on 09/03/20
Inspired to write about the play well museum

7

Seasons of Love #04

On the hospital grounds
There lies a café.
I always stop for a coffee.
Done sessions in there with my staff.
Stuck on the wall is this painting
Seasons with Love
Live each season with Love
Live each day with Love
Love thy neighbour as thy self
Can you recall a time when you had loved your neighbour
as yourself?
What did you do?

Moral Message
"You Shall love your neighbour as yourself"
There is no other commandment greater than this

Composed on the train on 12/03/2020
Inspired to write about the picture in the cafe

Joseph's coat of many colours #05
Gen 37:3

We all have friends at school or university.
We all have families and cousin.
Some of us have not got families.
Some are refugees or from poor families.
In the bible Jacob, Joseph's dad, liked Joseph
more than any of his children.
Joseph was his son of old age.
Joseph was able to interpret dreams
He interpreted his own dream and said
his father and brothers would bow down to him.
Jacob made Joseph a coat of many colours.
How do you think this made his siblings feel?
They became envious.
So they sold Joseph to a trader
who took him to Egypt..
What did his brother do then?
They took his coat of many colours
smeared it with blood and took it to Jacob.
Jacob was inconsolable.
The coat represented God's light of many colours
It was a depiction of Gods glory found in the third
heaven.
It also represents Gods righteousness emanating from
Joseph
Joseph and Jesus Christ have so many similarities
Isn't that amazing?
Somewhere around 150 various analogous traits.
Jacob favoured Joseph and gave him the coat as a gift.
As a result Joseph was envied by his brothers.
The brothers saw the special coat as an indication that
Joseph would assume family leadership.
What has this poem said to you?

Baby in a manger #06 # Saviour

At the front of the church
we have the table of communion.
We also have an altar.
Under the altar we create a manger
We have figures of the wisemen,
Mary the mother of the baby.
Joseph, Mary's husband.
Who is the baby in the manger?
Jesus our saviour.
Jesus being born in a manger signifies
that although Jesus is God, he left Heaven
to be born in a lowly stable.
Mary and Joseph were forced to have a baby
in a room for animals instead of a guest room.
They used a manger as a makeshift crib
for Baby Jesus
The Birth of Christ is the most famous bible story of all.
The accounts say Jesus was born in Bethlehem of Judea.
He was born amongst animals signifying humble
beginnings.
The shepherds were the first visitors.
So I would encourage you to find out what were the gifts
the wise men brought to Jesus
and what do they represent.

Moral Message
Jesus the Messiah came to this world to save "his people":
those who would believe in him.

Composed at home on 15/03/2020
Inspired to write about the manger

13

Feeding the multitude #07
#Compassion

The feeding of the 5,000 is reported by all four gospels

I was visiting the town of Canterbury.
My husband visits this pub each time I visit my son in
university.
The fish we ate reminded me of how Jesus fed 5,000
with two fish and five loaves.
The gospel of John reports the fish and loaves were
supplied by a boy.
When Jesus saw the large crowd he had compassion and
healed the sick.
Jesus message here is one of multiplication
that we can becomes fishers of men
by our actions of compassion to one another,
and by spreading the word of God and helping them to
salvation.
We should have compassion towards one another.
If we have food we can share this with friends who
might not have enough.
Have you shared your lunch with anyone you can recall?

Moral Message
To be compassionate for the needy and provide them
with the sustenance of God.

Composed on the train on 17/03/2020
Inspired to write about the fish in the restaurant

15

The Sea of Galilee 08 #Sea/Life #Allusion

The banner of love
has always hung at the church.
The octopus, star fish and fish
all remind me of the Sea of Galilee...
also known as Lake Tiberius
where Jesus walked on water and
calmed the storm.
It is also the lowest fresh water lake on earth
The dead sea is salty and is lower
So the sea of Galilee is the second lowest lake.
It is about 62 square miles.
The. Banner of Love:
The time and effort put in by the kids
The art and craft of all
The different colours light up the world
The blue signifies the sea.
The red heart signifies the blood of Jesus
The life beyond our imagination
The writing reminds us of our love for Christ
The different pieces the different months of the year
The different fabrics the different children's ideas
The Banner
God loves us all

Moral Message
Gods control over elements, including the chaotic sea.

Inspired to write about the banner in church
Composed on the train on the 19/03/20

17

The Lion of Judah #09
#Strength Isaiah 11:6

I went to Brentwood Theatre.
We saw the Lion of Nandia.
The symbol of the lion is used to represent different things.
It is a Jewish and national cultural symbol.
It is regarded as the symbol of the Israelite tribe of Judah.
According to the Torah
the tribe of Judah
are the descendants of Judah,
the fourth son of Jacob.
It heralds the lineage as one of the Kings.
Jesus was referred to as a Lion in Genesis.
This is a spiritual attribute of Jesus
as he is also the Lamb of God.
It shows he is as powerful and as majestic
as a lion,
and innocent as a sacrificial lamb.
What have you learnt about Jesus in this poem?

Moral Message
Lions are symbols of Leadership. Lion is considered the
king of animals. It is also a term representing Jesus.

Composed at home on 20/03/20
Inspired to write about Lion of Judah

King Solomon asks for Wisdom #10

Why did Solomon ask God for wisdom?
Do you remember a time you prayed to God?
A time you asked God for something specific?
Specific at the time of the Corona virus.
Corona virus did not affect children initially.
But suddenly when the Pandemic hit Britain
it affected children in different ways.
Children as young as babies contracted the virus
from their mother's womb.
I asked God for direction once.
God gave me an insight to write a faith book for children.
This happened in church
and I received confirmation at the same time.
Solomon asked God for wisdom in-order to rule the people.
"as who is able to govern this great people of yours" he said
The fear of the Lord is the beginning of wisdom
If we possess wisdom from God in our hearts and believe
it we will never perish.

Moral Message
King Solomon asked for wisdom so he can make good
decisions for his people.

That is very reassuring in the Pandemic season
Composed at home on 29/04/2020
Inspired to write about Wisdom

Let your light shine #11
#Enough John 8:12

The saying in the bible says:
Let your light so shine so they can praise your father in heaven
It goes further today. When you light a lamp
you don't leave it under the bed.
Light is the source of goodness.
It is illumination and intelligence.
It is the sun.
It's the avenger of evil forces and darkness.
It means doing things that make you feel free and peaceful.
Surrendering control,
Trusting my intuition,
Showing compassion and kindness to you
and others.
Believing the simple truth that I am enough.
It is about bringing light to the places that are dark.
Are you enough?
In the Bible Light means
Holiness, Goodness, Wisdom and Knowledge, grace hope
and Gods revelation,

Moral Message
Light has always been seen as a sign of holiness,
Goodness, knowledge, wisdom,grace, hope and Gods
revelation. Darkness is associated with evil.

Composed at home on 28/03/20
Inspired to write about The Light

23

Delilah and Samson #012 Lust and Trust

What does the story of Samson teach us?
Samson had the strength of a Lion.
Samson had a taste for the sweetness of honey.
Samson followed the proscription of a Nazarian's life:
No drinking alcohol or trimming his locks.
Samson had never used a razor on his hair.
Samson strength was linked to his hair.
Samson led the Israelites for twenty years.
Samson served as a final judge of Israel.
Delilah was portrayed by some as Samson's wife.
Delilah was described by some as the sister of Samson's wife.
Delilah was also described by some as a prostitute.
Delilah was also bribed by the lords of the Philistines
to discover the source of Samson's strength.
Delilah tried three times.
Samson's true love and downfall was Delilah.
Delilah coaxed Samson into revealing
that the secret of his strength was his long hair.
Delilah then took advantage of his confidence
to betray him to his enemies
Samson's power was sapped after Delilah cut his hair
They shaved his hair; he lost his strength
and he was captured by the Philistines
How long was Samson's Hair?
The message is not to reveal the source of your strength
even to your loved one.
Samson fell in Love with Delilah.

Moral Message
God wants to enable us to fulfil the calling he has given us.
Samson could further his mission as God gave him strength.

Composed at home on 31/03/20
Inspired to write about the story of Delilah and Samson

25

The Land of the Living #013

With all the chaos around the world
I cannot but wish and know
that I must see the goodness of the Lord in the land of
the living.
Land of the living means to be human:
to be awake or to be alive.
How many verses on the bible refer to the land of the
living?
This remind us if we trust have courage and wait upon
the lord we will receive.
We should expect something good is going to happen.
When you have that mindset
you are bound to look and believe
and look upon the Lord for his goodness.
Do you remember a time you were waiting
in expectation for something good to happen?
I always do and would encourage you to do the same.

Inspired to write about the land of the living
Composed on 02/04/20

Jesus rode a donkey 014 #Palm Sunday

This marks the beginning of celebrations of Holy Week
Jesus time of suffering, resurrection and death
happened during Holy Week.
Jesus riding the colt of a donkey is significant
as a donkey is seen as something not befitting a king.
It represents his few days before the last supper
and represents his passion.
Jesus demonstrated he is the messiah and king
Christians celebrate Jesus entry into Jerusalem on Palm
Sunday
The people there laid down their cloaks.
The people there also laid down branches of palm trees:
That is why we call it palm Sunday.
The people said, 'Blessed is he who comes in the name of
the Lord'.
This period represents a week of celebration known as
Holy Week.
Jesus rode on the colt of a donkey.
The donkey represented the Jews under the burden of the
law
What a contrast and message that Jesus portrayed in this
story:
His humility before the people.
What town did Jesus stay in before entering Jerusalem?
How many days did Jesus stay there before the Passover?

Moral Message
Jesus riding on a donkey signifies a humble king of Peace.
It symbolises arrival in peace compared to a war waging
king arriving on a horse.

Composed at home on 05/04/20
Inspired to write about Palm Sunday

29

Jesus rose from the dead #015
#Life will prevail

"He is not here he is risen from the dead"
Jesus tomb was a place I visited when I went to Israel.
It was a familiar place I could relate to.
There are lots of deaths happening around the world
in the COVID-19 pandemic.
But as Christians the message of Easter remains.
There is a special Easter service at the Garden Tomb in Israel.
We had a service at the Tomb and communion when we
visited the Garden tomb.
It's called the Garden Tomb Easter Service.
We believe in a resurrected Lord and his triumph over death.
This season reflects that despite the difficulties around
life will prevail.
Death and crucifixion is one station on our way to
resurrection.
This poem is so timely in this season
and I am thankful to God for this vision.
Life will prevail
Happy Easter in Advance everyone.

Moral Message
If we follow Jesus we too will have eternal life.

Composed at home on 08/04/2020
Inspired to write about the Garden Tomb in Israel

Noah's Ark 016 #Lessons learnt

What have you learnt from this season of the Pandemic?
What have you learnt at home now that you can't go to school?
What is different about not going to church?
What has happened at home that is different for you?
What if we loved each other more?
What if we gave each other space to be who we are?
What if we use the time to bond with each other?
What if we prayed and fasted together as a family?
What if we used the opportunity to learn about each other?
What if we used it to connect with each other?
What if the Lock Down is a period for reflection?
What if the period carried on forever?
What if we have still not learned from the experience?
We can cook different meals.
We can do some home schooling.
We can pray together as a family.
We can give each other space.
We can learn to see people for who they really are.
We can learnt a lot from people's energy.
We can see from how people behave when you are around them.
They want to box you into a corner.
Noah's Ark has taught us to live in the present.
Make the most out of it.
Noah's Ark

Moral Message
Noah's three deck ark represents the three level Hebrew cosmos in miniature -heavens, earth and waters beneath. God created the three level world as a space in the midst of the waters for humanity. Gen 6-8

Composed at home on 10/04/2020
Inspired to write about Lock down situation

33

Ten Commandments #017 Exodus 20

What is the best commandment?
You shall have no other Gods before me.
Love your neighbour as yourself.
Respect your father and mother
so your days can be long on earth.
So If we know this
why do we ignore these three commandments
as, if we respect and love our neighbours
they will follow our example. They may come to Jesus.
John 3:16 confirms that God so loved the world
that he gave his only son so that sinners might be saved.
The man in the picture reminds me of
an angel or father looking down at his children
and holding them close to his heart.
Thou shall not steal
Thou shall not commit murder.
So that was Gods way of testing us
so we have the fear of God with us
to prevent us from sinning.
What commandment is most significant for you?

Moral Message
The Ten Commandments are the first direct communication
between a people and God.

Composed at home on 11/04/2020
Inspired to write about 10 commandments

35

The Red Sea 018 Split poetry

The nations did not have the answers.
The Israelites were not sure where to go.
The Virus came unexpectedly.
The Egyptians were attacking the people.
The Virus was attacking human lungs.
God caused an East wind to blow on the sea all night.
This caused the sea to part and a pathway through the waves appeared.
The People were advised to stay at home.
God told Moses to hold up his hands over the pathway through the sea.
The sea was a wall on both sides of the path through the sea.
People were advised to keep 2 metres apart.
as social distancing will delay the spread.
The parting of the Red Sea by God is the most dramatic
and consequential occurrence in history.
The virus is also seen as the most dramatic pandemic to affect the world globally.
Pharaoh and his army thought they could follow the Israelites along the path.
So also the scientists and WHO had little or no knowledge of the Corona virus but
knew it was quite deadly.
God controlled the sea so that when Pharaoh's army tried to cross
God released the sea thereby exposing pharaohs army
and they drowned as the returning waters overwhelmed them.
So also the nations were affected by the virus with little or no knowledge of the underlying health issues and the impact it could have.
Moses and the Israelites crossed safely.
An action of God at the time of the exodus
foreshadows all nations being saved if they have faith and are baptised.
This story is death and the rebirth of salvation.

God spoke to Moses #019
The Burning bush

How old was Moses when God spoke to him?
Why did God speak to Moses?
Why was the bush not consumed by the fire?
What is the significance of the burning bush?
Why did Moses have to lead the Israelites?
Which town were they fleeing from?
Who was the leader of the Israelites?
What did God say to Moses?
Do you remember a time when God spoke to you?
Why would God not speak to us?
Why did Moses have to remove his sandals?
I recall God speaking to me.
I was sitting in Church one Sunday
When God inspired me to write a Faith book
God also sent a manifestation.
This was a sign of three Children in the Church
I am grateful for the opportunity to share the story
through the lenses of a child.
God wants his children to come to him.
But before we approach him we have to cleanse ourselves.
The other message here is there are times
when I could be going through a challenge or storm
yet you feel very focused and unphased.
This is the presence of God.
So this is the reason why there was a fire.
But the bush was not consumed by the fire.
The Burnish Bush

Moral Message
The burning bush conveys the nature of God Deut 4:24
God is a consuming fire.
God is a holy God so anything unholy will be consumed or
destroyed by Gods holiness.

Inspired to write about a time God spoke to me
Composed in my room at home on 27/04/2020

Moses was put in a basket #20

Pharaoh declared that all Hebrew boys should be killed.
He fears the Hebrews might become too powerful.
Jochebed is scared:
she may not be able to protect her child
so she puts him in a basket and lets him float down the
River Nile.
Pharaoh's daughter finds the basked stuck in the bulrushes
with a baby in it.
She adopts him.
He is raised as an Egyptian.
After Moses is weaned, Pharaohs daughter names him Moses,
taken from the word 'masah'.
Moses is the prophet most often mentioned in the New
Testament.
He delivers the Jews from slavery in Egypt.
Can you remember a time anyone has attempted to protect
you?
Was this from harm for good?
What was the reason why?
We understand Moses was protected from
being killed by Pharaoh.
What a dramatic turn:
His own daughter knew the child was a Hebrew
But she never told her Dad, Pharaoh.
Can you trust anyone?

Moral Message
Pharaoh of Egypt had ordered all Hebrew baby boys were
to be slaughtered at birth.
Moses mother gives birth and decides to hide her son.

Composed at home on 18/04/2020
Inspired to write about Moses in the basket

41

Jonah and the whale #021

Do you recall a time you disobeyed anyone?
Your mum, Teacher or Nan?
Do you recall what happened?
How did that make you feel?
Did you ponder on it at all?
Did you regret your actions?
Jonah disobeyed God
by running away after disobeying Gods order to go to
Nineveh.
Why did Jonah run away?
He ends up on a journey on a ship –
and guess what? there was a storm.
You hear of storms but God will save you and I
from any storm in life but we have to be obedient
to our, mum, teacher or nana.
The sailors on the ship thought the storm happened
because of Jonah. So they threw him overboard.
Jonah was swallowed by a whale during the storm.
That must have scared the life out of him.
That tells us if we disobey,
our actions may catch up with us later.
Jonah prayed to God from the stomach of the whale
which reminds us of being in the midst of a storm.
The fish vomits Jonah on to land and Jonah goes to Nineveh.
"What an interesting act from God" I thought.
What's the message in this story to you?

Moral Message
A Person Cannot run away from Gods Plans.

Composed at home on 25/04/2020
Inspired-to write about Jonah and the whale

43

Mary Anoints Jesus feet #022 John 12:3

In the town of Bethany,
Jesus had raised Lazarus from the dead.
Jesus was having supper with Lazarus
and his sisters, Martha and Mary.
Martha had opened her doors to Jesus.
Mary, her sister, sat at Jesus's feet.
Martha was distracted as she prepared a meal.
She complained that Mary wasn't helping her.
But Jesus said 'Mary has chosen the better part,
and it shall not be taken from her.'
Listening to the teachings of Jesus is more important than
cooking.
The word of God fills you up like nothing else.
The words are spirit and life. Meaning eternal life.
Mary took a pint of a very expensive perfume
made from pure nard
and poured it on Jesus feet.
And she wiped Jesus feet with her hair.
Spikenard was a very expensive aromatic oil.
Anointing can make you do supernatural things:
A means of health and comfort.
As a token of honour.
As a symbol of consecration.
It is also seen as an ordinance of consecration.
Mary was described as a sinner in the bible.
We are all sinners and can gain comfort from Jesus
who has washed our sins away.
In what way are you sinful?
The message here is not to get too distracted by life.

Moral Message
Be prepared to be used by Jesus, Put your Faith in God.

   Composed at home on 26/04/20
   Inspired to write about Martha sister of Mary
   Copyrights reserved by Sabinah Adewole.

Fall of Jericho #23

The stone walls date back to 8000bc
The walls represent the first military barricades..
The walls are at least 13 feet high and are backed
by a watch tower at least about 28 feet tall.
The walls fell after the people of Israel marched
once daily for six days around the city.
On the seventh day they marched seven times
and blew their trumpets ▢ ▢
The walls collapsed and fell outwards
thereby creating steps for the Israelites
to climb up into the city.
Joshua's army conquered the city killing everyone except
Rahab
who had helped them to get into the city.
She and her family were saved.
The city was set alight.
Why was Rahab and her family saved?
What were the Israelites carrying when they marched
around the city of Jericho?
Joshua and his army destroyed other towns and he became
the ruler of Canaan.

Moral Message
God wants to break down the walls of our heart and let
himself in

Composed at home on 21/07/2020
Inspired to write about Jericho walls
Copyrights reserved by Sabinah Adewole.

47

Rebekah had faith in God #24

She is the wife of Isaac.
She is mother of Jacob and Esau.
She is daughter of Bethuel the Aramean.
She went to the well with her servant.
She met Isaac and asked who he was.
She dismounted from her Camel.
She covered herself with a veil.
She was brought by Isaac into the tent of his deceased mother, Sarah.
She married Isaac and he loved her.
She was married in the tent and this is mirrored in modern Jewish marriage rites.
Rebekah is also known as Rivka, Ribqa or Rapqa
She and Isaac prayed to God for children.
She became pregnant after twenty years.
She was uncomfortable during her pregnancy
She sought advice at the yeshiva of Shem and Eber.
She was told she was carrying two nations in her womb.
Rebekah is the second or third woman to feature in the Bible
Rebekah means Captivating, Knotted and Cord
Who does Rebekah remind you of?
Which quality of Rebekah do you admire?

Moral Message
Both of her sons suffered setbacks in life because she favoured one above the other.
We should let our children go on their faith journey and trust that God loves them more than we do.

Composed at home on 29/04/20
Inspired to write about Rebekah

Eve #25 #Overcoming #Temptation #Obedience Gens 1-5

Eve is the first woman in the bible.
She has been depicted as the person who brought sin to human kind by her actions in the garden of Eden.
Adam and Eve were warned by God not to eat the forbidden fruit.
He told them if they ate it they would die.
But Eve was tempted by the snake who asked her to eat the fruit.
"But God said we will die if we eat the fruit." Eve said.
The snake said they would not die
but would gain knowledge of good and evil.
Eve ate it and gave some to Adam.
Adam and Eve realised they were both naked.
So they sewed fig leaves together to cover themselves.
Because of this God knew they had disobeyed him.
God removed them from the Garden.
Do you remember a time you were tempted to do something?
Temptation can come to you in many forms.
You hear two voices in your head.
Most times one voice is good and the other one can be manipulative.asking you to do something like lying for example.
And you know that could get you into trouble.
So when next you are faced with a dilemma in life,
pause for a minute.
Explore the options. Find a way around it.
Speak to a friend or teacher.
And then go on from there,
but don't act on your first instinct.
I am sure God is with you all the time.
He is there with you on this journey.

Moral Message

Obey and Attain Knowledge in relation to good and evil. Without faith in God without believing what he says, he is fully capable of enforcing his word.

Composed at home on my 28 th wedding anniversary
On the 02/05/2020 Lock down Anniversary

52

Deborah #26 #Judges 4 -5

Deborah is the only female judge mentioned in the bible.
She is the wife of Lapidoth.
She inspired the Israelites to attack the Canaanites who oppressed them.
The Israelites are victorious.
Even though you may have been trapped or locked into captivity by cultural and gender prejudices,
God expects us to break through these barriers.
I attended a women's retreat this year
and it was called 'Deborah Arise'.
Now it makes sense what this means.
Have you ever found yourself in situations
where it seems nothing you tried is working?
Sometimes this is considered deliverance
or a Deborah anointing to set you free.
Deborah was a judge in Israel
She rendered her judgements under a palm tree
between Ramah in Benjamin and Bethel in the land of Ephraim.
Deborah is described as a compassionate leader
and the only female judge in the bible in a lawless country before they got their first king.

What are your thought on Deborah being the only female judge?

Moral Message
Women can be in Godly Leadership.

Composed at home on my anniversary
Inspired to write about Deborah

53

54

Jezebel 027 # wickedness #vengeful

Jezebel the daughter of Ethbaal:
She married king Ahab of Israel.
She encouraged him to worship the Tyrian god, Baal Melkart.
Most of the prophets of Yahweh were killed at her command.
She was a Phoenician princess
who married King Ahab and became Queen.
She continued to worship the nature god Baal Melkart.
Most of Yahweh's citizens and prophet Elijah despised her.
She was later killed by the prophet Elijah.
She is described as a morally unrestrained woman,
shameless and impudent.
Why was Jezebel designed this way?
Why did she continue to misuse her power?
Why did she continue to worship the god of nature?
By manipulation and seduction
she misled the saints of God into sins of idolatry
and sexual immorality.
There are people with whom you may come into contact
and God would reveal to you they are not right for you.
They continue to throw daggers and
you know you are not making progress.
So we need to make sure our friendships are right for us.
If we feel pressure to do wrong things,
then those friendships need to be monitored.

Moral Message
Don't use your influence to turn others away from God.

Composed at home on 03/05/2020
Inspired to write about Jezebel in the bible and
how wickedness could lead you astray

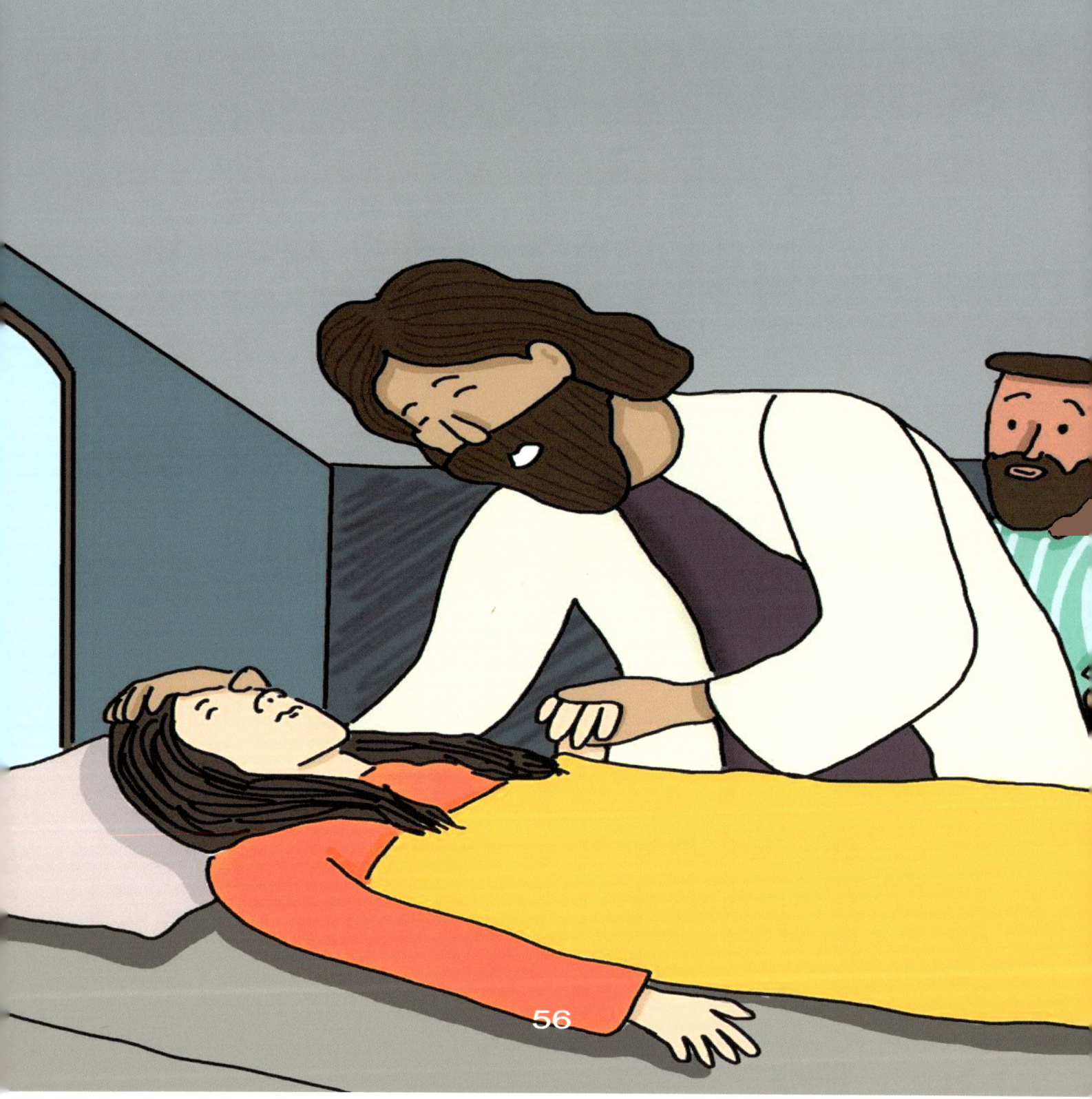

56

Jesus raises a girl from the dead and heals a sick woman #028 #healing

We are in the middle of a pandemic across the globe.
Children are witnessing death figures on our TV screens.
Populations are decreasing by numbers.
People of all ages are dying in hospitals across the globe.
So the thought of Jesus raising a dead girl
and healing a lot of people comes to mind.
He healed the sick woman and many others.
COVID-19 has claimed so many.
But we can also believe that Jesus has healed so many.
I know one or two who contacted the virus and have been in recovery.
The British Prime Minister, Boris Johnson, contracted it,
and is recovering in Downing Street.
A woman who was bleeding for 12 years came to Jesus.
Jesus healed her and others because of her faith.
Do you believe that you can be healed?
She showed her faith by going to Jesus.
Jesus showed compassion by healing her
because he felt sorry for her.
He rewarded her for her faith.
Trust and believe you will be healed.
Our God is a healer.
Have you prayed for anyone and
received healing for them through your faith?
I have .... and so have others.
All our nations need healing.
We need to go to him in prayer.
The woman went to Jesus and that was her faith in action.

Moral Message
Jesus deals with a double miracle Death and Diseases, for the disciples to be given confidence in Jesus power.

Inspired to write about the woman that was healed
Composed at home on 17/05/2020

58

The significance of the boy #29
#The hungered are fed

Reminds me of a time I visited Israel in 2018.
A boy had come up to me in front of the church to sell
magnets.
This boy had come up to Jesus when he was in front of
a gathering crowd of 10,000 or more.
With the pandemic we have a lot of people struggling
and receiving food from food banks
and the government and charities are helping to feed the
hungered.
What can you do to support your neighbour in a time like
this?
You have drawn rainbows to support the NHS.
This is the only other miracle story to appear in all four
gospels.
John is the only one to mention the boy or lad in his story.
He is the original human source for the five loaves and two
fishes
This is a miracle that Jesus performed
and I am aware this is Day 25 of the Ramadan season.
Andrew, Peter's brother, had informed Jesus:
'Here is a boy with five barley loaves and two fish to feed
the crowd.'
Jesus asked the crowd to sit down.
There were Five thousand men there.
Jesus shared the barley loaves and two fish amongst the
people
who had gathered and were seated.
The remaining scraps were packed into twelve baskets.
Children were among the crowd of people that followed Jesus.
Children would be in the company of their family members.
But the boy was standing very close to Jesus.
He was from the poorer class of society.

Barley is cheaper than wheat and is for the poorer class.
The poor commonly ate barley loaves.
It was not uncommon for children in those days
to become a young enterprising salesman
to sell to people who have gathered together.
And till this day children gather in Israel
to sell trinkets or bottled water to pilgrims
who have shown up for religious reasons just like I did.
Jesus' crowds were bound to attract such kids
and Andrew and I spotted one.
What an amazing experience I have just shared with you.
I am blessed
Jesus places value on the little boy and uses him to do
something big.

Moral Message
Sharing Jesus love with someone can mean filling any kind
of need, not just a spiritual one.

Composed at home on 19/05/2020
Inspired to write about the little boy in the crowd

61

Let the Children come on to me #30
#Rivalry #Disciples rebuke Matt 19:14

Jesus wanted to pray and lay hands on the children.
Their families had brought the children to Jesus.
The disciples felt they were bothering Jesus and rebuked
them.
When you attend for communion in church
the Vicar lays hands on children and prays for them
if they have not been confirmed.
Why do you think the Disciples rebuked the families?
Infants were also brought to Jesus so that he might touch
them.
It was believed there was a political agenda.
The disciples felt the kingdom of God was the earthly
kingdom of Israel.
It was to be brought forth by mighty men and not children.
Jesus saw the potential power in children
who were dependent on one another. That is God.
Jesus saw the spiritual understanding and humble faith of
children who can receive the supernatural kingdom of God.
How does that make you feel?
Would you want to meet Jesus if you had the opportunity?
This controlled strength combined with a genuine attitude
and openness renew people to Jesus.

Moral Message
Jesus knew the disciples did not understand what was
important to him.
The story brings out a real morality and the virtue in kids.

Inspired to write about the meaning of the actions
of the disciples
Composed at home on 21/05/2020

Innocence #31 Matt 18:1-4

God wants us to become like a little child to enter the
kingdom of God
The disciples came to Jesus and asked him
'Who is the greatest in the kingdom of heaven?'
He called a little child and had him sit amongst them and said
'Whoever humbles himself like a child is the greatest in the
kingdom of heaven.'
The faith God looks for is humble, teachable and trusting.
So have you had a time you felt the presence of God in your
life?
Are your parents religious?
Do you go to a Christian school?
Have you been touched by the Holy Spirit?
Have you been through a baptism ceremony?
How old were you at the time?
These questions would help you to understand what God is
looking for and is why he believes you have to be like a child
to be the greatest in the Kingdom of heaven.

Moral Message
God is able to lead us and his word can lead us to victory.
God supports a humble person when he/she is waiting.

Composed at home on 22/05/20
Inspired to write about humility in the child

The Rod of Wisdom imparts correction
#32 #Discipline #Prov 29:15

The rod of correction was a term
used by the shepherds in the fields.
Teach your child what to do and they never depart from it..
Parents have a role to lead their children on the right roads
to take.
Parents show their children what choices to make.
And let the children understand the consequences of their
actions.
A child is reprimanded and the mother is disgraced
by an undisciplined child.
A child that is not disciplined disgraces the mother.
The Hebrew of the word rod is "shebet"
Foolishness is bound in the heart of a child.
As the rod of correction drives it far from him.
A foolish son is the heaviness of his mother.
It would seem the Mother's had a role to play
in the children's best behaviour.
Growing up in a single parent family
mother's do not necessarily have to use the rod.
As the children would understand by the look of the eyes.
Have you had to be disciplined by mum?
Can you recall how this happened?
What did mum say or do?
Or what did Dad say to remind you?

Moral Message
Is not for corporal punishment, however, was used by
shepherds in the fields and also a way of reminding parents
job to lead a child as to what choices they have and
the consequences of those choices.

Inspired to write about the rod and staff they
comfort me
Composed at home on 24/05/2020

The Good Shepherd #033 John 10:1-21

The thief cometh that they might steal, Kill and destroy.
I came that they may have life and have it abundantly
'I am the good shepherd, the good shepherd lays down his life for his sheep.
I am the good shepherd, I know mine own, and mine own know me.
Even as I know him my father knowers me and I lay down my life for the sheep.
And other sheep that I have, which are not of this fold I must bring,
and they shall hear my voice and we shall become one flock, one shepherd.
I give unto them eternal life, and they shall never perish and no one shall snatch them out of my hand.'
There was division amongst the Jews
as they did not believe or understand his words.
The Jews took up stones again to stone him.
What does this story teach us?
When we care for our neighbour as our self
we become good shepherds taking care of our flock.
The opposite to that is if one sheep goes missing what would you do?
We go after it and find the lost sheep as we are one flock and one shepherd.
Jesus lays down his life for his sheep and is described as the Good Shepherd.
I hope this has helped someone today.

Moral Message
Each one of us is precious before God. The shepherd is a good shepherd who loves and cares for his sheep.

Composed at home on 25/05/2020 (Bank Holiday)
Inspired to write about the Good shepherd

69

The Prodigal Son #034 #Luke 15:11-32

Jesus shares the parable with his Disciples, Pharisees and others.
The father has two sons.
The younger son asks for his inheritance.
This son is described as prodigal extravagant and wasteful.
He squanders the money and becomes destitute.
He decides to return home and begs his father to accept him as a servant.
This poem is created on a day
when the Minnesota police killed a black man in broad daylight.
No one deserves to die like that.
To the eldest son's surprise, the son is welcomed back by his dad with celebration and a welcome party.
The older brother is envious and refuses to participate.
The father reminds the older son:
'You are ever with me and all that I have is yours.
Your younger brother was lost and now he is found.'
This is the third parable about the cycle of redemption:
'The lost Sheep', 'The lost Coin.'
This implies the father was hopefully watching for his sons return.
The father asks the servants to dress him in robes, put a ring on his finger, sandals on his feet and slaughters the fatted calf.
So the moral of the story is that we are all precious before the Lord
No one deserves to die.

Moral Message
God is ready to receive sinners who come to him in repentant faith. Believers should not be jealous when God blesses and saves those who come to him in repentant faith.

Composed at home on 27/05/20
Inspired to write about the Prodigal son

70

71

Go and make disciples of Nations
#35 Matt 28:19-20

God teaches us to obey him in all things
and he is saying all authority has been given to him
and he baptises us in the name of the father, son and Holy
Ghost.
A disciple is someone who seeks to obey his master, Jesus,
and follow him.
A true disciple would ask what would Jesus do?
In other words Jesus would like you to have a mindset
of knowing the word
and know what to do when you are in a difficult situation.
A disciple learns from a teacher.
An apostle is "one who is sent off".
He or she goes and delivers the teachings to others –
a messenger who is sent.
The narrow meaning of apostle is those linked closely to Jesus
Most Christians hold this dear whether they practise it or not.
This refers to all corners and all peoples of the world.
So we have a duty to go and be a disciple of Jesus
but the choice is yours to become an apostle or disciple.
Which would you prefer to be a teacher, messenger or
follower
Or all three and why?
I encourage you to have a think
about what it would have been like to be a disciple of Jesus.

Moral Message
The authority and task on what to do was clear and given
by Jesus to his disciples
This was a clear mandate given by Jesus to "go and make
disciples of all nations"

Composed at home on 28/05/2020
Inspired to write about the disciples

73

Who is King David? #036

He was born around 1000 BC.
He was a descendant of Judah as well as Ruth.
He was promised by God that his children will rule Israel forever.
He is a strong unassuming shepherd who rules.
He became Gods choice to replace Saul as king of Israel.
He is humble and self-possessed.
He gained fame as a Musician.
First he was known as the 'sweet singer of Israel',
the source of poems and songs,
some of which are collected in the book of psalms.
His humility shone through as a child's.
He killed the giant Goliath with a stone flung from a sling.
He declined to use Saul's royal armour.
He is Israel's second king and built a small empire.
He conquered Jerusalem and made it Israel's Political and Religious centre.
He defeated the philistines who never threatened Israel again.
He aroused Saul's Jealousy, and so Saul plotted to kill him.
He is the youngest son of Jesse.
Until this day he is remembered by Jews everywhere.
He reigned for 40 years
in one of the most prosperous periods in Israel's history.
He was not born into royalty but he rose to found a dynasty.
He became a central figure in Christianity, Judaism and Islam.
His era was looked back on as the golden era.
He is so successful because
he weaves the religion of God into the very life of the people.
David had many wives although only eight of them are named.Bathsheba was David's favourite wife
of the eight wives five are mentioned only once
and the other three figure prominently.
Would you like to have met King David?
Having read about King David what do you admire about him?

Moral Message
If size mattered to David (as it did to the Israelites) he would not have had the courage to take on Goliath. It's your heart, courage and commitment that matters.

Composed at home on the 31/05/20
Inspired to learn more about King David

Finding him in the temple #37

Is also the story known as 'Christ among the doctors'.
He accompanied Mary and Joseph to Jerusalem
amongst relatives and friends.
Jesus was in Jerusalem because
Jewish boys went on a pilgrimage at the age of 12.
This was at the time of celebrating the Passover.
When the people in his group started out for home,
Jesus lingered on and stayed in the temple.
He was found conducting his father's business – teaching
in the temple.
His parents went to Jerusalem every year for the feast of the
Passover
Jesus was in the temple in discussion with the elders
who were amazed at his learning.
Jesus said to Mary:
'Why is it you sought after me? did you not know I must be
in my Father's house, about my father's business?'
This was the first time we see Jesus lose his temper and
show his human side
Jesus is quite unique in this poem as one of the youngest in
the temple and how his confidence shone.
Can you remember a time you displayed such confidence
and bravery?
How many days did it take Mary and Joseph to find Jesus
in the Temple?
What does this story teach us?

Moral Message
An angel told Mary and Joseph of Jesus purpose before he
was born, and yet they still did not understand why Jesus
stayed behind in the temple. Jesus was spending
time with his true father. At aged 12, Jesus knew his
purpose was to save people from sin.

Composed at home on 04/06/2020
Inspired to write about Jesus in the temple

78

The healing of the Leper #038
#Matthew 8:1-4

When he came down from the mountains
There was a crowd gathered that followed him.
A man with leprosy came and knelt down before him.
"Lord if you are willing you can make me clean"
Jesus reached out and touched the man
'I am willing' he said 'Be clean.
Don't tell anyone but go show yourself to the priest
and offer the gift Moses promised as a testimony.'
What does the story teach us?
It reminds me of our world today needing healing
From hurts, Anger and Racism.
Our world is kneeling in unison.
Our lives were taken with a knee gesture.
Our Lord is asking us to kneel before him.
Crowds are gathered.
Our crowds are kneeling in unison
Jesus reached out his hand and
touched the man.
Immediately he was healed to the blacks.
It needs to be stripped off.
Jesus is willing to heal the world of this leprosy.
We need to reach out to him.
We need to ask him to heal our world.
He is always willing to clean the world of this leprosy
of Racism.
What is the gift he is referring to in the story?
Why did he send the man to the priest?

Moral Message
Jesus was willing to heal the leper as leprosy was regarded
as an unclean disease.Jesus was not supposed to come close
to him let alone touch him. The leper reached out to Jesus.

Composed at home on 9/06/2020
Inspired to write about the Healing of the Leper

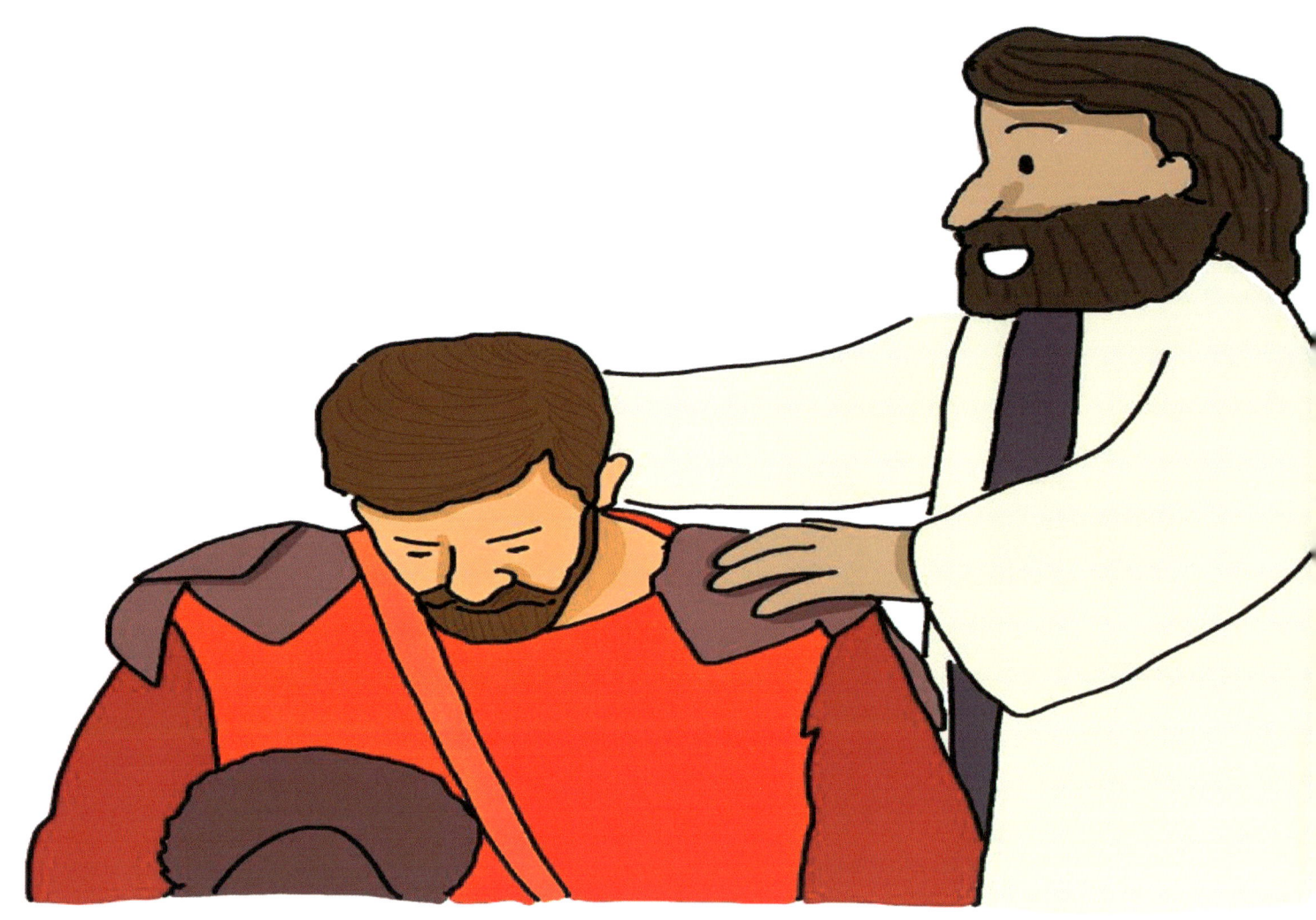

The Faith of the Centurion #039
Luke 7:1-10

Teaches us of a strong confession of faith in Christ.
He teaches us that Christ's word is as good as his deed.
He can accomplish whatever he pleases
just by saying the word.
How reassuring is that to us as children of God?
How secure does that make you feel?
That you know by having faith and believing
In Christ
we get what we ask for and believe the word.
He entered Capernaum
There was a Centurion's servant.
His master valued him highly.
He was sick and about to die.
The Centurion did not think he was worthy
for Jesus to come under his roof.
He was also a man in authority.
Jesus was amazed at his faithfulness.
'I have not found such faith in Israel,' he said.
Then the man who had been sent
returned to the house and found that the servant had been
healed.
I once had to pray for Boris during the pandemic
and everyone joined me in prayer
and he was healed.
So I believe in miracles.
How did the story make you feel?

Moral Message
A lesson of faith. Jesus said he had not found anyone in
Israel with such great faith.

Composed at home on 14/06/2020
Inspired to write about Faith

The unforgiving servant #040
#Forgiveness

Teaches us to learn to forgive others
as we are forgiven by God.
Do you recall a time you were forgiven?
What did you do at the time?
I recall a vivid time in my life.
I was forgiven by my husband at the time.
You can forgive but not forget.
However it is better if you could do both.
Peter asked Jesus how many times should he forgive.
In return Jesus said 70 times 7.
The lord forgave the servant his debts of 10,000 talents.
But the servant did not forgive his servant that owed
one hundred denarii.
When the Lord learnt of this
he delivered the servant to his tormentors until he paid back.
So will the Lord do to you if you don't forgive your brother
from your heart for his misdeeds.
So we must try and forgive each other as the Lord's Prayer
teaches us to do.
"forgive us our trespasses, as we forgive those who trespass
against us."

Moral Message
Use your God given gifts in the service of God, and take
risks for the sake of the service of the kingdom of God.
failure to use the gifts will result in negative judgement.

Composed at home on 26/06/2020
Inspired to write about forgiveness

84

Nicodemus #41 you must be heard before judged John 3

Nicodemus was a Pharisee,
a member of the Sanhedrin.
He wanted to know more
of what Jesus taught.
Very inquisitive.
Mentioned thrice in John's gospel.
He reminds the members
you must be heard
before you are judged.
Why did he come to Jesus at night?
He had done some research.
Jesus performed miracles
and said
No one can see the kingdom
unless they are born again.
This message has stuck with
Christians and is hidden in their
hearts.
God did not send his son into the world
to condemn it.
But he sent his son
to save the world through him.
Do not feel condemned.
Whoever believes shall not perish but
have eternal life
as God has come to save the world.
Have you ever felt this way?

Moral Message
It is important to be baptised in the name of the father, the son and the Holy Spirit.

Composed at home on 20/06/2020
Inspired to write about Nicodemus

86

Hadassah #42 # The book of Esther

She was a bright young Jewish woman.
She was sent by God to save her people from destruction.
She was also known as Queen Esther.
King Xerxes ruled the Persian Empire and was searching for
a wife.
All the eligible girls in the kingdom were summoned to the
palace.
Mordecai, her cousin, told Esther not to admit to being Jewish.
All the young maidens were brought to the palace.
They were given beauty treatments for a year within the
palace before they were brought before the king for him to
pick a wife.
Esther was scared because Jews
were forbidden to appear before the king.
If the King discovered she was Jewish she would be killed.
Jews were hated and mistrusted amongst the people.
Hadassah therefore changed her name to Esther.
When she was brought before the king
he was charmed by Esther and chose her to become his queen.
During her time as Queen, an evil man named Haman
convinced the king to kill all the Jews.
When Mordecai found out he sent word to Esther.
Esther was afraid to appear before the king as
the law stated a person must be summoned.
If someone were not summoned, yet appeared
The king might ignore them and they would be executed.
However, if the king accepted the person
he held out his sceptre towards them.
Mordecai convinced Esther that she had been put in a high
position by God
in order to save her people from destruction.
Queen Esther commanded all the Jews, including herself, to
fast for three days.
After this, she went before the king.

The king was pleased to see his queen. He held out his sceptre.
Esther told him everything and Haman was put to death.
An edict went out from the king about the Jews.
Now they could defend themselves from attack and persecution.
In this way Esther saved her people.
What was the role of Mordecai in this story ?
Is Esther or Mordecai the saviour in your opinion?
Why was Haman put to death?

Moral Message
God raises people into certain positions , because he has a plan for them and will use them to help more of his people.

Composed at home on 26/07/2020
Inspired to write about Hadassah
Copyrights reserved by Sabinah Adewole

89

The woman of Samaria #043
#John 4:4-25

This is a story that teaches us how Jesus breaks
Cultural Lines
Religious lines
Gender lines
Ethnic lines
by engaging with the woman of Samaria.
He was a Jew and Jews did not mix with Samaritans.
They are referred to as half breed renegades.
They were hostile to each other.
But Jesus was not afraid to break barriers down and mix
with people.
He cared for people more than their divisions.
It was culturally unacceptable for a man to speak with a
woman privately.
The Samaritans were mixed ethnicity and religion.
Jesus reveals he is the messiah she has been waiting for.
The woman runs off to inform the village of what she has
heard and learnt.
What do you think the reaction of the villagers will be when
they hear her story?
The villagers ask Jesus and he disciples to hang around for
two days.
What did they do?
Jesus and his disciples engage with the Samaritans on an
intimate level despite massive cultural divides.
What have you learnt from this story?

Moral Message
The hope of the word of the Lord that entered into her
world of brokenness to reveal a new Kingdom full of living.

Composed at home on 28/06/2020
Inspired to write about the Samaritan woman

91

Who was John the Baptist #044

The son of Zechariah and Elizabeth in the Bible.
The forerunner before Jesus Christ.
Estimated to have been born six months before Jesus.
The Angel Gabriel appeared to Zechariah and said
that Elizabeth would have child.
Zechariah did not believe and was muted.
Elizabeth was barren due to old age.
John baptised many people in the River Jordan.
The name John was given by an angel of God.
He was believed to be a second cousin to Jesus.
He baptised Jews in the River Jordan on the confession of
their sins.
He lived in the desert until the beginning of his ministry.
John baptised Jesus in the River Jordan.
When Jesus was baptised this started the beginning of his
ministry.
Jesus declared no greater man than John had been born of a
woman.
He was beheaded in 31AD.
Herodias daughter, Salome, danced for Herod.
As a reward she asked for the head of John the Baptist on a
platter and her wish was granted.
Mormons believe that John was ordained by an Angel
at 8 days old to prepare a way for Jesus.
Why did Herodias ask for Johns head on a platter?

Moral Message
Jesus regarded John as a burning and shinning lamp and
willing to rejoice in his light.

Composed at home on 30/06/2020
Inspired to write about John the Baptist

92

93

The Tower of Babel #045
Gen 11:1-9 final

Represents the origins of the beginning of the multiplicity
of languages.
God was upset that humans had built a city and high tower.
It was built in the land of Shinar (Babylonia) after the
Deluge.
They all spoke the same language.
God said 'If as one people speaking the same language
they have begun to do this,
then nothing they plan to do will be impossible for them.'
So God confused their language to curb their progress.
Humans became divided
because they could no longer understand each other.
Adamic language is believed to have been spoken before
by Adam and Eve in the garden of Eden.
The Adamic language, according to the Jewish tradition
is recorded in the midrashim
and some Christians believe it existed.
Nimrod states the tower is built in Babel
and he is the leader of those that built the tower.
However the Bible does not state this fact.
Nimrod first built the cities of
Babylon, Uruk, Akkad and Kalneh, in Shinar.
as recorded in Gen 10:10.
Archaeologists believe that Eridu in Mesopotamia
is the most probable site of the tower of Babel.
The remains of a Ziggurat in Babylon
is thought to be the inspiration for the tower of Babel.
What have you learnt from this story?
Would you have liked to visit The Tower of Babel?
What language can you speak?

Moral:
Pride goes before a fall. The people of Babylon
wanted to be like God, we must humble ourselves before
God and others.

Composed at home on 03/07/2020
Inspired to write about The Tower of Babel

Day 1   Day 2   Day 3

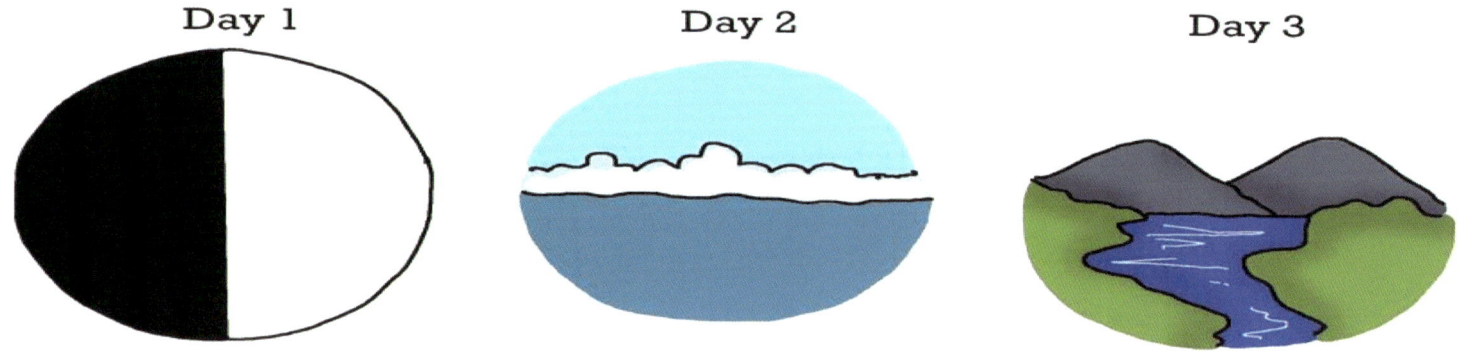

6 Days of Creation

Day 4   Day 5   Day 6

The Story of Creation #046
Were Animals Created before humans ?

Imagine being there at the onset of creation
God created the heavens and the earth
What next? you will think.
The earth was formless.
There was no globe ☐ ☐ or earth as we know it.
Darkness we understand was over the deep waters.
That reminds me of the Titanic.
The spirit of God comes to the rescue hovering over the sea.
And then God created light and
it became lit - what a contrast from dark to light.
It took Six days to create the world.
On the seventh day, God rested.
Day one light was created can you imagine being in the dark?
Day two the sky was created. Can you imagine no sky?
Day three there was dry land, seas, plants, and trees.
imagine an empty world – what will it be like?
Day Four the sun, stars and moon were created how
marvellous is that?
Day Five God had a plan -creatures that live in the sea (fish)
and creatures that fly (birds) were created.
God is very creative and selective. What do you think?
Day Six Animals that live on land were created
and finally humans were created in God's own image.
So were animals created before humans?
Day Seven God finished and rested.
This day became known as a special holy day.
What day is this?
What day would have been your best day and why?
If you had a choice would you reverse the order of Creation?

Moral Message
God is responsible for the creation of the world, Christians believe religion explains the reason it was created.

Composed at home on 08/072020
Inspired to write about Gods Creation

99

How Did Daniel Survive the Lion's Den? #047

Daniel name means "God is my Judge"
He is the hero of the book of Daniel.
He interprets Dreams and receives apocalyptic visions.
King Darius's ministers were jealous of Daniel.
They persuaded the king to issue a decree:
'No prayers to any man or god for thirty days except to Darius.
Anyone who breaks this rule will be thrown into the lion's den.'
Daniel was devoted to God and could not bow down to any other god.
Therefore, he prayed to God in secret, and disobeyed the ruling.
But his enemies were watching Daniel and reported him to King Darius.
Darius was fond of Daniel and tried to save him,
but Daniel's enemies would not be persuaded.
They insisted Daniel should be punished.
So Daniel was thrown into the den of hungry untamed lions and the door was sealed.
Daniel has a close relationship with God.
He knows God better than any other person on earth.
He spent hours daily with God and cherished his presence.
He craved to know, worship and be with God.
He lived in God's presence and lost himself in his presence and forgot himself and he did this as a tradition.
Although King Darius does not want to do it, he agrees to throw Daniel into the lion's den.
The following morning King Darius went to the den and called to Daniel.
Daniel said an angel had come and closed the lion's mouths.
The King was overjoyed and gave orders for Daniel to be lifted out.
No wound was found because he had trust in his God.
Then King Darius decreed that all his kingdoms must worship Daniel's God.

The bible teaches us that God will never leave us or forsake us Heb 13:5
We can never defeat the devil on our own merits he will outsmart us so we need Jesus
The only way to win is through Jesus.
Why did Daniel survive the Lions in the den?

Moral Message
God leads us to a challenge because He is with us and has given us the ability to overcome it.

Composed at home on 09/07/2020
Inspired to write about Daniel

Why did Jesus carry the Cross
#048 John 19:17

Jesus carried the cross until he could carry it no more.
Simon of Cyrene helped Him with the cross
when it became too heavy.
Jesus carried the cross for 1.5 km
That is about from Collier Row to Romford.
Have you had to carry something so heavy?
How did that make you feel?
Jesus had to go through suffering for you and me.
Simon was recruited by the soldiers to help carry the cross.
John's is the only gospel to mention this in the bible.
It is not clear why Jesus had to do this.
Jesus is known to have fallen
at least three times on his way to Calvary.
This is represented by the stations of the cross in the
Catholic Church.
We can liken Jesus carrying the cross to
a burden or trial that one must endure.
This term can be used lightly or seriously.
To carry a cross means to carry the burden of the church.
Jesus carried the sins of the world.
We carry the burden of our unrepented sins.
Also, if we love Jesus we help to carry his burden.
But this is described as a good burden to bear.
Can you imagine what it felt like?
Have you seen anyone wearing or carrying a cross?
Now I understand why they wear a cross, do you?
Jesus was beaten with a staff, spat at and scourged.
He wore a crown of thorns on his head.
The accused would carry the cross beam to the place of
crucifixion.

Moral Message

Even though Jesus couldn't carry his own cross, He is the only one who could help you carry yours. There is no greater love than Jesus, for he died for us.

Composed at home on 14/07/2020
Inspired to write about the crucifixion

105

The Devil in the Desert #049 Matt 4 #Temptations

Jesus was in the desert fasting.
He fasted for forty days and forty nights,
alone and Hungry.
The devil appeared to him at his weakest
and said 'If you are the son of God,
change these stones into bread.'
Jesus replied, 'Man shall not live by bread alone
but on the word of God.'
The devil took Jesus to the Holy City,
to the highest point of the temple
and said 'If you are the son of God, throw yourself down.
Angels will save you.'
Jesus replied, 'do not test God.'
The Devil took Jesus to a high mountain,
where he could see the kingdoms of the world and said:
'Bow down and worship me and I will give you all this.'
Jesus replied 'Go away, Satan. Worship is for God alone.'
The devil then left Jesus
and the angels of God came to attend to him.
If you hold fast to the word of God
then no one can make you stumble.
Do you recall a time
when you have been tempted
to do anything against your will?
What did you do at the time?
Jesus was tempted three times
but he dismissed the devil and the devil left him.
So Jesus did this by using the scriptures to respond to the devil
How would you resist the Devil?

Moral Message
Hold fast to the word of God, then no one will be able to cause you to stumble.

Composed at home on 16/06/2020
Inspired to write about the temptations on Jesus

The Ten Virgins #050

The parable of the Ten Virgins
illustrates that we have to be prepared
for we do not know when the
Bridegroom, Jesus, will arrive.
Five wise virgins lamps were filled with oil.
Five foolish virgins lamps were not as full
so they ran out of oil.
What do you think will happen to them?
Spiritual perseverance is key.
It is a parable that relates to both men and women,
as we all need to be prepared
for we never know the right time the groom will attend
the wedding party to meet his people.
Who is the groom in this parable?
The oil symbolises goodness, warmth and safety.

Moral Message
The call for 'readiness' in the face of uncertain times in the
second coming.
Described as a watching parable it makes the same point
about readiness in a preceding parable about men.

Composed at home on 17/07/2020
Inspired to write about the 10 Virgins

"Children, obey your parents in everything, for this pleases the Lord." The Good News: Children follow your parents will. God has given them the tools to help you grow into a faith-following servant of the Lord- the Bible tells us so. "Give thanks to the Lord- for he is good, His love endures forever"

A note from the Author

Thank you for reading my book hope to continue my journey with you in my next book

-Sabinah